AN OFFICIAL U.S. SPACE CAMP BOOK

THE U.S. SPACE CAMP®

★★★ **BOOK OF** ★★★

ASTRONAUTS

Anne Baird

FOREWORD BY DR. N. JAN DAVIS
INTRODUCTION BY JAMES B. ODOM

CHAIRMAN, ALABAMA SPACE SCIENCE EXHIBIT COMMISSION

MORROW JUNIOR BOOKS   NEW YORK

To my dear children, Tracey Allen, Edward Baird,

and Amanda Baird, with thanks for their constant love and support.

And to my big brothers, Bill and Jim Breukelman,

who are always there for me.

ACKNOWLEDGMENTS

As always, many people contributed their time, talent, energy, and resources to this book, in particular, Edward O. Buckbee, former director of the U.S. Space and Rocket Center and U.S. Space Camp, whose encouragement of young people's aspirations for space-related careers continues unabated; and Dr. N. Jan Davis, whose life as an astronaut should inspire future space pioneers to work, as she did, to make those dreams come true.

Richard E. Allen, Jr., former general manager of the U.S. Space and Rocket Center, and Dr. Tommie R. Blackwell, the center's director of education, gave invaluable assistance. Lisa Vest, program manager at Space Camp, was very helpful.

Special thanks to James Hagler, curator of the U.S. Space and Rocket Center, and to Frederick I. Ordway III. Their advice and assistance with space photographs and paintings added greatly to this book. Thanks also to photographer David Graham, who captured so beautifully the wonder and enthusiasm of the Space Camp trainees as they learned about space and astronauts!

I am especially grateful to Colonel Guion S. Bluford, Jr.; Dr. Franklin R. Chang-Diaz; Colonel Mark C. Lee; Dr. Mamoru Mohri; Colonel R. Mike Mullane; Dr. George D. Nelson; and Dr. Sally K. Ride, who shared some of their thoughts and experiences as astronauts with the readers of this book. Mrs. Edward C. Corrigan, the mother of S. Christa McAuliffe, added special insight into her daughter's brief but unforgettable space career.

From NASA's Astronaut Office at the Lyndon B. Johnson Space Center, I am extremely grateful to both Lucy Lytwynsky and Barbara Present. And to Dr. Allen E. Puckett, friend, first reader, and former chairman of Hughes Aircraft, my thanks, as always.

No list of acknowledgments would be complete without thanking Andrea H. Curley, senior editor at Morrow Junior Books, and Faith Hamlin, my agent. The launch of *Astronauts* would not have been possible without them.

PHOTO CREDITS

Permission to use the following photographs is gratefully acknowledged:

Culver Pictures, page 8; David Graham, pages 7, 19, 44; Griffin-Hudson, page 46; NASA, pages 1, 3, 11, 12, 13, 15, 16, 18, 20, 22, 23, 24, 25, 26, 29, 30, 31, 33, 34, 35, 37, 38, 39, 40, 42, 43; NOVOSTI/SOVFOTO, page 9; U.S. Space Camp/Bob Gathany, page 28.

The name SPACE CAMP is a registered trademark.
Copyright © 1991 Alabama Space Science Exhibit Commission.

Book design by Anne Scatto and Martin Zanfardino/PIXEL PRESS

Printed in Hong Kong by South China Printing Company (1988) Ltd.

1 2 3 4 5 6 7 8 9 10

Library of Congress Cataloging-in-Publication Data
Baird, Anne.
The U.S. Space Camp book of astronauts/Anne Baird; foreword by N. Jan Davis; introduction by James B. Odom.
p. cm.
"An official U.S. Space Camp book."
Includes bibliographical references and index.
Summary: Biographies of America's astronauts with a history of the space program.
ISBN 0-688-12226-4 (trade)—ISBN 0-688-12227-2 (library)   1. Astronauts—United States—Biography—Juvenile literature.
2. Astronautics—History—Juvenile literature. [1. Astronauts. 2. Astronautics—History.] I. Title.
II. Title: U.S. Space Camp book of astronauts.   III. Title: United States Space Camp book of astronauts.
TL789.85.A1B35 1995   629.45'0092'2—dc20   [B]   95-10634   CIP AC

OVERLEAF: Buzz Aldrin, one of the first two human beings to walk on the Moon, poses for a historic lunar portrait. Reflected in his visor are the lunar module, scientific equipment, and Neil Armstrong, who took this picture.

Foreword

As long as people have inhabited this Earth, there have been explorers willing to take risks for discovery and exploration of the unknown. Our own country was discovered by such pioneers, who overcame phenomenal obstacles to make their discoveries. Following a great and long history of explorers, astronauts today continue the natural progression of exploration by pushing the far frontier of space.

It is truly amazing to think of the development of technology in this century that has culminated in space travel. As an astronaut, pilot, engineer, and American, I can affirm

that our exploration into the far reaches of space is a result of the determination, vision, dedication, and perseverance of many men and women. Their breakthroughs in technology are evident in our everyday lives and constantly remind us of the many facets of the space program that advance other scientific and technical frontiers.

We must go forward and continue to explore and dream. It is vital for our country's future to pass this legacy to future generations. *The U.S. Space Camp Book of Astronauts* inspires children as it informs them about those of us who have been fortunate enough to have flown into space. By learning that astronauts have excelled at math and science, have set goals, and have been greatly influenced by parents and teachers, hopefully the young people

who read this book will realize that they, too, can be explorers of the future and find an exciting and fulfilling adventure in the space program. I encourage them to dream, as all astronauts have done, and then to build the foundation to make those dreams come true.

DR. N. JAN DAVIS

NASA Astronaut
Mission Specialist on STS-47 (Spacelab-J) and
STS-60 (Spacehab and the Wake Shield Facility)

Introduction

I've spent nearly forty years in the space industry. I wouldn't trade any of those years for the treasures of the world. In fact, I would sign on for forty more.

Why? It's really quite simple. I believe our greatest space achievements are still ahead. Our only limitations would be a lack of imagination and a fear of hard work.

The U.S. Space Camp Book of Astronauts does a splendid job of documenting how, since 1961, astronauts and cosmonauts have conquered those limitations. Their story is one of men and women who don't wonder if space travel is possible. Instead, they put

their trust in scientists, engineers, and visionaries such as Dr. Wernher von Braun and Sergei Korolyov. Imagination and hard work take over. Rockets are built to propel our space travelers above Earth and, in some cases, on to the Moon. Together, they dream—face down their limitations—and then make their dreams come true.

What's most exciting to me today is how *the dream* I shared with countless thousands forty years ago is still alive in our young people. I have the honor and privilege of spending time with the ones who attend U.S. Space Camp and Space Academy programs. Their eyes light up when they talk about the space station, returning to the Moon, and colonizing Mars. They and others will carry the torch of space exploration into the next century and beyond because they too will not set limitations, and they too will not be afraid of hard work.

The stories of the courageous space explorers in this book will be an inspiration to all future explorers—whether *you* aspire to accomplish your goals with a computer, a test tube, or a space voyage to Mars.

JAMES B. ODOM
Chairman, Alabama Space Science Exhibit Commission
Former NASA Associate Administrator for the Space Station

Contents

Space Camp Astronauts Meet the Real Thing

On the Training Floor of the U.S. Space and Rocket Center's famous Space Camp in Huntsville, Alabama, busy campers are engrossed in hands-on astronaut training. Space Camp is a place where people go to find out what it takes, and feels like, to be a NASA-style test pilot or astronaut. In the mock-up of the Space Shuttle *Columbia,* Apple team's Flight Crew rehearses their Shuttle mission. They will follow a Space Camp script based on actual NASA missions. Seated in the flight deck, the team's commander and mission specialists wait for their Mission Control teammates to start the run-through. What's the holdup?

Suddenly, their counselor, Allyson, appears at the top of the ladder ascending from the middeck below. "Take five," she says in an excited voice. "There's someone here who wants to meet you!"

It's George D. "Pinky" Nelson, former astronaut. Dr. Nelson flew three Shuttle flights between 1984 and 1988, logging 411 hours in space. He is known for the extravehicular activity (EVA) in which he helped capture and repair a malfunctioning satellite called Solar Max, then return it to orbit. He helped prove that people can work in space.

"This looks familiar," he says, climbing into the flight deck. He studies one of the camper's mission scripts and nods approval.

"Looks like what *we* said just before lift-off. You sure this thing won't take off? I've got a meeting with your camp director, so I better get out quick! Work hard, now. Some of you might be astronauts for *real* one day." He waves and disappears down the ladder.

"Ready up there?" yells Allyson. "Mission practice!"

"Roger," calls the mission commander. "We're ready. . . ."

When the rehearsal is over, the children ask Allyson if she knows a lot of American astronauts. "Not really," she admits. "But I've read a lot about them in books."

"Any favorites?" asks one of the children.

"Sure. Alan Shepard. John Glenn. Gus Grissom. Neil Armstrong. John Young. Sally Ride. Guion Bluford. Christa McAuliffe. But also some of the Russian cosmonauts, like Yuri Gagarin and Valentina Tereshkova. And there are tons of interesting astronauts flying *right now.* I've got lots of favorites!"

"What makes them want to go into space?"

"Good question!" says Allyson, pleased. She gathers the group around her, and they settle down comfortably on the floor. "To answer it, we're going to have to go back a bit.

"People have dreamed of flying into space for thousands of years. . . ."

Former astronaut George Nelson checks out the flight deck of Space Camp's mock-up of the Space Shuttle *Columbia*. Nelson flew his second mission aboard the real *Columbia* in 1986.

Ballooning to Blast-off

"In 1783," she says, "the Montgolfier brothers made the first free flight across Paris, in a basket hanging from a huge silk balloon. The two Frenchmen had discovered that when they filled the balloon with heated air and gases, it became lighter than the air surrounding it and would fly. For the first time, humans were able to travel above the Earth. It was awesome!"

By 1865, French author Jules Verne took his readers even higher in his book *From the Earth to the Moon.* The science-fiction writer imagined a journey in which three men flew to the Moon in a bulletlike spacecraft shot from a cannon. The story was so believ-

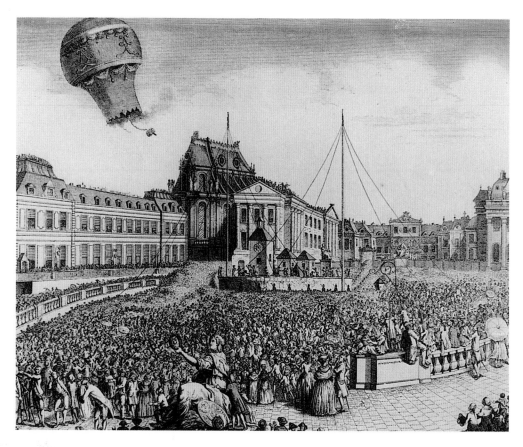

Joseph-Michel and Jacques-Etienne Montgolfier launch the second flight of their hot-air balloon at the palace of Versailles on September 19, 1783. The French royal family and over 130,000 spectators cheer as the balloon rises over the palace, travels for eight minutes, and then lands safely in the woods nearby. Aboard with the men are a rooster, sheep, and duck, whose survival helps prove that flying is safe for animals, too!

The first human being in space, cosmonaut Yuri Gagarin, rockets to glory aboard the *Vostok 1* capsule on April 12, 1961. Nicknamed Gaga and the Space Swallow by his jubilant countrymen, Gagarin will also be given a new title, created for him by Soviet Premier Nikita Khrushchev: First Hero Cosmonaut.

able that many early rocket scientists wanted to make space travel a reality. This didn't happen, though, until almost a century later.

In the years after World War II, which ended in 1945, the United States and the Soviet Union were bitter enemies. They were also bitter rivals, with both superpowers trying to be the first in space.

On October 4, 1957, the USSR succeeded. It launched *Sputnik 1,* the world's first artificial satellite, into Earth orbit. Three and a half years later, they did it again. On April 12, 1961, a Soviet cosmonaut, Major Yuri Gagarin, became the first man in space. Not only did he leave the Earth, he orbited it in his *Vostok 1* capsule, then safely parachuted down near the Volga River, ninety minutes later. He returned to a hero's welcome in Moscow, and to worldwide celebrity.

"You have made yourself immortal," Soviet Premier Nikita Khrushchev told him, and he was right. With the launch of *Sputnik 1,* followed by the flight of Gagarin, the Soviet Union launched the space age.

The Mercury Astronauts

"The United States was shocked at being beaten into space," Allyson continues. "Americans wanted the U.S.A. to be number one in science and technology again."

On July 29, 1958, President Dwight D. Eisenhower signed the National Aeronautics and Space Act. Two months later, NASA, the civilian space agency, was born.

On December 17, 1958—fifty-five years after the first successful heavier-than-air flight of the Wright brothers at Kitty Hawk, North Carolina—NASA announced its first manned spaceflight project: the Mercury program. It would last from 1958 to 1963 and consist of six successful solo flights. Its goal was to put a man into orbit, study his reactions to spaceflight, and recover him safely. But first, NASA had to find men willing to become America's space pioneers. It wasn't easy!

An early thought was to recruit arctic explorers or deep-sea divers—almost anyone who loved adventure and who wasn't afraid to take a chance. But NASA eventually came up with a better idea. Astronaut candidates would be chosen from an elite pool of 508 military test pilots from the armed forces, who tested the country's fastest, newest aircraft to see whether they were safe. NASA wanted the bravest and the best.

NASA's requirements for its first astronauts were strict. Each candidate had to be:

- an active military test pilot, with a minimum of 1,500 hours of flight time (Since women weren't military test pilots in those days, all early astronauts were men.)
- only five feet, eleven inches tall or shorter (If they were taller, they wouldn't fit into the space capsule.)
- 180 pounds or less (Extra weight would add to the load to be lifted into space.)
- under forty years old
- a college graduate, with a background in engineering

Only 110 of the 508 military test pilots qualified under these rules. And of the 69 men NASA interviewed, only 39 volunteered for the job. NASA decided that was plenty. They put those volunteers through the most rigorous testing possible to find a handful of finalists.

On April 9, 1959, the seven astronauts, named the Mercury Seven, were presented to the world: Alan Shepard, Virgil "Gus" Grissom, John Glenn, Scott Carpenter, Walter Schirra, Gordon Cooper, and Donald Slayton. All of them would fly; one of them would die in the line of service; one would wait sixteen years to launch into space. But the Mercury Seven set standards of courage and excellence for all future astronauts.

NASA's first group of astronauts, the Mercury Seven, pose for the press in 1959. From left to right, front row, are Walter M. Schirra, Jr., Donald K. Slayton, John H. Glenn, Jr., and M. Scott Carpenter. In the back, left to right, are Alan B. Shepard, Jr., Virgil I. "Gus" Grissom, and L. Gordon Cooper, Jr.

Alan B. Shepard, Jr.

"The first American in space was Alan Shepard," says Allyson. "He rode in a capsule called *Freedom*. The whole world watched and listened as he blasted off!"

Born in East Derry, New Hampshire, on November 18, 1923, Alan Shepard was the son of an army colonel. But he chose to attend Annapolis, the naval academy. He earned a bachelor of science degree in 1944. After graduating, he served on a navy destroyer in the Pacific. In 1945, he married Louise Brewer, with whom he had two daughters. He earned his wings in 1947 and served as a naval pilot aboard aircraft carriers in the Mediterranean. In 1950, he went to the United States Navy Test Pilot School, where he became one of the elite naval test pilots. He attended the Naval War College at Newport, Rhode Island, graduated in 1957, and was assigned to the staff of the commander in chief of the Atlantic Fleet. In 1959, he became a Mercury astronaut.

Competition among the astronauts for the honor of being the first American in space was friendly but intense. On February 21, 1961, NASA announced that the difficult choice had narrowed to Shepard, Grissom, or Glenn. Three days before launch, the secret was out. Commander Alan B. Shepard, Jr., would be first—backed up by John Glenn.

On May 5, 1961, Shepard suited up. At 5:14 A.M., he entered the elevator that carried him up the side of the sixty-five-foot-tall Redstone missile to the capsule on top. There, he lay on his special contoured couch and was strapped in for blast-off.

Mechanical difficulties and poor weather conditions delayed the launch repeatedly. But at 9:34 A.M., the Redstone rocket ignited and shot Shepard's capsule 116 miles above Earth—like a manned bullet. With him rode America's hopes for its future in space.

For the first time, an American experienced weightlessness in space. It was "pleasant and relaxing," Shepard later reported. "And it had absolutely no effect on my movements or

The Mercury Seven pose again during a desert-survival training exercise in Nevada. The grubby-looking astronauts wear Arab-style clothing made from strips of parachute cloth. From left to right are Gordon Cooper, Scott Carpenter, John Glenn, Alan Shepard, Gus Grissom, Walter Schirra, and Donald Slayton.

efficiency." This was great news for NASA, which had wondered whether an astronaut could function in the microgravity of space. (Because of that concern, Mercury capsules were designed to fly automatically, even though they were flown by some of the best test pilots in the world.)

Although the view from the capsule's window was spectacular, Shepard had little time to enjoy it. He flew on autopilot until after *Freedom* separated from the rocket booster that thrust it into space. But then, unlike Yuri Gagarin, *he* took

Alan Shepard is rescued from the Atlantic Ocean by a navy helicopter at the end of his flight. A-OK! THE U.S. IS IN SPACE, *Life* magazine will report shortly.

over, using manual controls intended as backup in case the automatic systems failed. NASA wanted to know whether a pilot could control a spacecraft in space. Shepard could and did. He returned the capsule to autopilot only after he had positioned it, manually, for reentry.

Fifteen minutes after lift-off, the ride was over. Shepard and *Freedom* splashed down in the Atlantic Ocean, 302 miles from the launch site. A navy helicopter picked them up and brought them aboard the aircraft carrier SS *Lake Champlain*. Shepard returned to an exuberant welcome from the sailors, a ticker-tape parade in New York, and a White House ceremony during which he was awarded a NASA medal by President John F. Kennedy. Telegrams of congratulation poured in.

Although his flight was suborbital and he did not circle the Earth as Gagarin had done, Shepard actually flew his spacecraft and had some control over his mission's destiny. Best of all, he put the U.S. in space! Twenty days after the flight of *Freedom,* President Kennedy announced that America would land a man on the Moon, and return him safely to Earth, before 1970.

Commander Shepard returned to Houston and became chief of the Astronaut Office. He expected to fly one of the first Gemini two-man missions but was grounded because of a serious inner ear infection he developed, called Ménière's disease.

In 1968, however, he returned to active astronaut duty after an operation cured his condition and, in 1971, commanded the *Apollo 14* lunar mission. He was the only member of the crew with any space experience. And that was only fifteen minutes!

On August 1, 1974, Alan Shepard retired from NASA and the navy to work as a private businessman. But as president of the Mercury Seven Foundation, he continues to encourage young future astronauts. "I am excited about the youngsters of today," he has said. "There are still new frontiers for your generation to explore."

John H. Glenn, Jr.

"John Glenn loved airplanes!" Allyson tells the Apple team. "When he was growing up, his bedroom was filled with models of biplanes he built. And he zoomed around his backyard, his arms spread like wings, pretending he was flying."

The only son of a plumber named Herschel Glenn and his wife, Clara, John Glenn was born July 18, 1921, in Cambridge, Ohio. The family moved to the nearby town of New Concord, and John spent the next twenty years there. Nobody could have predicted that a boy who graduated from New Concord High School, who attended local Muskingum College, and who married a girl he had known since the age of three would one day leave not just New Concord, but the Earth.

Glenn was a well-rounded young man. In high school, he was an honor student and president of his junior class. Though not a natural athlete, he lettered in football, basketball, and tennis. His future wife, Annie, cheered him on.

In September 1939, when John and Annie entered Muskingum College, World War II had begun in Europe. By 1940, with Germany occupying France and at war with England, it was impossible for Glenn to ignore the world beyond New Concord any longer. Believing that the United States would soon be drawn into the fight, he earned his license as a civilian pilot. Five months later, on December 7, 1941, the Japanese attacked Pearl Harbor, and America plunged into war. John dropped out of college, enlisted in the marines, and married Annie.

Though he hadn't wanted to make the military his career, by the end of World War II and the Korean War, Glenn was one of the best combat pilots the marines ever had. But his toughest fight was yet to come—the struggle to become an astronaut. Like many pilots, he loved flying the fastest, most powerful airplanes in the world. Now he wanted to fly higher. But reading NASA's requirements for becoming an astronaut, he discovered he didn't qualify! He was too tall (six feet), too heavy (208 pounds), and too old (at thirty-seven, he would be one of the oldest candidates); plus, he wasn't a college graduate!

Undaunted, he set out to conquer each obstacle. It has been said that he tried to shrink by walking around at night with a pile of books strapped to his head. (Whether this worked or whether he just slouched, his official NASA height is five feet, ten and a half inches.) By relentless exercise, he dropped his weight to 168 pounds. Though an older candidate, his strength and determination equaled that of younger men. And while he lacked a college diploma, the courses he took in the Marine Corps were equal to a college degree.

Chosen as one of the Mercury Seven astronauts in 1959, Colonel John H. Glenn, Jr., piloted America's first orbital flight three years later, on February 20, 1962. His entire mission, from start to finish, was broadcast worldwide over radio and TV.

Traveling at five miles a second aboard *Friendship 7,* the astronaut circled the Earth three times in less than five hours. During his first orbit, he described tiny glowing

particles, "like fireflies," streaming past the window of his spacecraft. (Later, it was discovered that the particles were ice crystals and flakes of paint from the capsule's exterior.) He ate applesauce squeezed from a food tube to prove that humans could swallow in microgravity. When the automatic flight control system faltered, he took over the controls and flew *Friendship* manually.

During his final orbit, NASA feared that the heat shield protecting him from the intense 3,000° F heat of reentry had come loose. The shield held, however, and *Friendship 7* splashed down with a sizzle into the Atlantic Ocean. There, it was recovered by cheering sailors aboard the USS *Noa.* Everybody breathed a sigh of relief.

"That was a real fireball," Glenn reported with a grin, but "my condition is excellent."

After his fiery return to Earth, Glenn received a hero's welcome that surpassed even that for Alan Shepard. He addressed a joint meeting of Congress and was feted by the United Nations. Newborn babies were named after him, and *Friendship 7* was installed at the Smithsonian Institution in Washington, D.C. Still, he remained a modest man. In an address to Congress, he shared the credit for his successful space journey with the thousands of people who had made it possible.

Glenn retired from NASA in 1964, the first astronaut to do so. In 1965, he left the Marine Corps. He was a business executive until his election to the United States Senate in November 1974. The first astronaut in the Senate, he still serves there.

John Glenn was once asked during an interview for *Life* magazine why anyone would risk his life to go into space. Why not do something less dangerous? "We've got to do it," he replied. "We're going into an age of exploration that will be bigger than anything the world has ever seen. If a man . . . takes the dare of the future, he can have some control over his destiny. That's an exciting idea to me."

The Gemini Astronauts

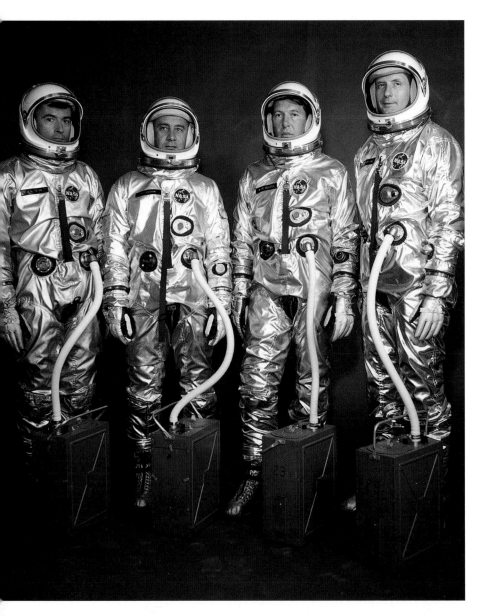

Two pairs of Gemini astronauts, John Young and Gus Grissom (left) and Walter Schirra and his partner, Thomas Stafford (right), wear space suits connected by hoses to their life-support-system packs.

"Mercury astronauts flew alone. They thought of themselves as pilots," says Allyson, "even though they had little control, at first, over spacecraft launched by ballistic missiles and guided by computers. In the next NASA program, Gemini, which means 'twins,' *two* astronauts flew in the spacecraft. They worked together as a team."

The brief Gemini program, lasting from 1965 to 1966, was a bridge between the Mercury and Apollo programs. The Gemini astronauts' first goal was to prove that human beings could survive and work in space for at least two weeks—the time NASA thought a lunar mission would take. A second goal was to show that one space vehicle could find another in space, and dock with it. If they could do those things, then Apollo astronauts, building on the Gemini experience, should be able to land on the Moon before 1970, as President Kennedy had promised.

Gemini capsules, like those of Mercury, were bell shaped but bigger and twice as heavy. With two astronauts lying side by side, it was a very tight fit. Perhaps that was why the first Gemini astronauts, Gus Grissom and John W. Young, were among the smallest men in the corps.

Virgil I. "Gus" Grissom

"When Gus Grissom was picked as one of America's first astronauts," Allyson tells her team, "a reporter found his former scoutmaster and asked, 'Do you remember Gus Grissom?'

"'Yes,' said the scoutmaster. 'But I'm mighty surprised he volunteered for such a mission!'"

The shy astronaut was the first to tell this story. The smallest of his group, at five feet, seven inches, Gus Grissom was easy to overlook. But he was tough and determined. Though deeply patriotic, he never thought of himself as a hero. "I'm not the hero type," he said.

Born on April 3, 1926, in Mitchell, Indiana, Gus wasn't the timid boy his scoutmaster remembered. He camped on his own and regularly slipped off to the nearby stone quarries to swim. When World War II broke out, he tried to enlist in the U.S. Air Corps but was rejected because he was too young. He applied again when he was eighteen and spent his wartime service as an aviation cadet. After earning a mechanical engineering degree from Purdue University, he rejoined the air force. He married and had two sons.

During the Korean War, Grissom flew 100 combat missions, for which he was highly decorated. Returning home in 1952, he became a jet pilot instructor. He joined the astronaut corps in 1959.

After Alan Shepard made his suborbital flight, it was Grissom's turn. On July 21, 1961, Lieutenant Colonel Virgil I. Grissom roared into space in *Liberty Bell 7.* The fifteen-minute Mercury mission went well. After splashdown, however, everything went wrong. The capsule's escape hatch blew too soon, and the craft sank. Grissom nearly drowned before he was pulled from the sea by a chopper. Later, his helmet was found floating beside a fifteen-foot-long shark!

Though NASA never blamed him for the accident, Gus Grissom felt bad about losing his spacecraft. The space agency showed their confidence in him by making him command pilot of the first manned Gemini flight. On March 23, 1965, he became the first American astronaut to go into space twice.

Teamed with Captain John W. Young, a rookie from the second group of astronauts, which was chosen in 1962, Grissom showed his sense of humor. He named their spaceship *Molly Brown,* after the heroine of a Broadway musical called *The Unsinkable Molly Brown*!

By the time they went up, no American had been in space for nearly two years. Soviet cosmonauts, meanwhile, had logged 507 hours in space, compared to 54 hours for NASA's astronauts. Only five days before *Molly Brown*'s launch, cosmonaut Alexei Leonov took the world's first spacewalk.

Grissom and Young's flight marked a turning point for NASA. A stunning series of ten Gemini flights, including Grissom's, paved the way for the Apollo lunar landings.

The crew of *Gemini-Titan 2*, Gus Grissom and John Young, prepare for mission practice at the Mission Control Center at Kennedy Space Center. Astronauts rehearse every detail of their flight for many months before they actually launch.

Though it looked like a Mercury capsule, the Gemini spacecraft *relied* on pilot control, instead of just permitting it. This made Grissom happy. He wanted to be a pilot, not a passenger! During his successful three-orbit flight, he fired the capsule's rocket thrusters to change orbits and did other maneuvers to prove the Gemini spacecraft's readiness for rendezvous in space.

Grissom's growing reputation as America's most experienced astronaut earned him a new assignment: command pilot for the first three-man Apollo flight. Some thought he might be chosen as the first man to walk on the Moon.

A young visitor studies the story of Gus Grissom in the Astronaut Hall of Fame in Titusville, Florida. Though small in stature, Grissom was a giant when it came to courage. He was one of the first American astronauts to lose his life in the space program.

Lift-off of *Apollo 1* was scheduled for February 21, 1967. Accompanying Grissom on this historic flight was Lieutenant Colonel Edward H. White II, who took the first American spacewalk during the 1965 *Gemini 4* mission. The third member of the trio was Lieutenant Commander Roger B. Chaffee, who was looking forward to his first spaceflight.

None of them rose any higher than the tip of the Saturn rocket—218 feet above Kennedy Space Center's Launch Pad 34.

On January 27, a few weeks before launch, the astronauts entered *Apollo* for a final dress rehearsal. The spaceship would operate entirely on its own power, not using any outside sources, to make sure that everything was working before the crew flew into space.

Dressed in their space suits, helmet faceplates down, the astronauts lay in a row on their contour couches. The escape hatch was bolted shut; the cabin pressurized. For the next five hours, they practiced procedures they knew by heart.

Suddenly, fire exploded inside the cabin. Despite frantic efforts to rescue them, the astronauts were dead within seconds—probably from smoke inhalation. Later, it was determined that a short circuit in the cockpit's wiring may have started the blaze. The cabin, filled with highly flammable pure oxygen for the astronauts to breathe, burst into flames at the first spark.

Grissom, White, and Chaffee were America's first spacemen to be killed on duty. Their tragedy shook NASA and the U.S. badly. But the astronauts themselves would have wanted the space program to continue.

Grissom had once said, "If we die, we want people to accept it. We are in a risky business, and we hope that if anything happens to us, it will not delay the program. The conquest of space is worth the risk."

The terrible loss of the three astronauts did delay the program. For nearly two years, more than 1,500 investigators worked to find out what happened, and NASA made important changes in the capsule and space suits so that such an accident would never happen again. But the program did not *stop*. On October 11, 1968, a new crew of three vaulted into space. And in less than a year, the United States landed men on the Moon....

The Apollo Astronauts

"The purpose of the three-man Apollo program," says Allyson, "was to land men on the Moon—before 1970. Apollo's astronauts worked together as never before. They had to if they hoped not just to land on the Moon but to return to Earth!"

John Young, commander of the *Apollo 16* lunar landing mission of April 16, 1972, takes a joyful leap from the Moon's surface as he salutes the American flag. The lunar module *Orion* is on the left. Next to it is the lunar roving vehicle, which Young will later drive at its top speed of 10 MPH.

The spaceship for this incredible journey was *very* complex. Astronauts would learn to fly two different spacecraft: the command module (CM) and the lunar module (LM). They would live and work in the CM during their eight-day trip to the Moon and back. Piloted by the CM commander, it was to keep orbiting the Moon while the other two astronauts flew down to the lunar surface and then back to the spacecraft in the LM.

Following the disastrous *Apollo 1* fire of 1967, three unmanned, then four manned, Apollo missions tested the improved spacecraft and the new fireproof space suits. Astronauts tested the LM and practiced the intricate rendezvous and docking maneuvers that would be critical to a safe lunar landing and return to Earth.

Gradually, the astronauts drew closer and closer to the Moon. During *Apollo 10*—the last flight before the Moon landing—Thomas P. Stafford and Eugene A. Cernan flew their lunar module to within nine miles of the lunar surface—and set the stage for the triumph that made the United States number one in the space race at last: *Apollo 11*'s Moon landing.

Neil A. Armstrong

"Neil Armstrong loved planes so much that he flew before he could drive a car," says Allyson. "On his sixteenth birthday, he earned his pilot's license. But he had to bicycle to the airfield, because he didn't have a driver's license!"

Born on his grandfather's farm near the small town of Wapakoneta, Ohio, on August 5, 1930, Neil was the oldest of Stephen and Viola Armstrong's three children. By the time he was six, he was crazy about planes. He built model airplanes and conducted experiments in the basement with a home-built wind tunnel.

He was a hard worker. His first job was cutting grass at a local cemetery for ten cents an hour. Neil was only seven. When he turned fifteen, he took a forty-cents-an-hour job before and after school to earn money for flying lessons. At Wapakoneta High School, he excelled at science and math, went out for football and basketball, and played the baritone horn in a four-man jazz combo he formed.

The navy gave him a scholarship in 1947 to study aeronautical engineering at Purdue University. Two years later, he was ordered to Pensacola, Florida, for flight training. By the time he earned his wings at age twenty-one, the Korean War had started. During his tour of duty he flew 78 combat missions and was known as a hot pilot who was cool under pressure.

After the war, he left the navy and returned to Purdue to finish his engineering degree. He married Janet E. Shearon, and they had two sons.

After Armstrong graduated from college, he went to work for NASA as a civilian test pilot for the legendary X-15 rocket plane. This plane flew faster than the speed of sound and so high (over fifty miles up) that eight of its pilots were given astronaut wings!

Armstrong had no interest in becoming an astronaut at first, since he was already flying the hottest experimental rocket plane of the time. But as NASA's launchers boosted other pilots higher into space, he changed his mind. Joining the second group of astronauts in 1962, he became the first civilian pilot in American space history. And on March 16, 1966, with Colonel David R. Scott, he launched as command pilot for *Gemini 8.* Their goal: to do the first U.S. docking in space, with an orbiting rocket stage called *Agena.*

After a successful docking, the linked spacecraft spun wildly out of control. Armstrong reacted swiftly and decisively. He undocked *Gemini* from *Agena,* fired its reentry rockets, and brought the craft safely home for an emergency splashdown. This quick action helped earn him the most prized assignment of the Apollo period: commander of *Apollo 11,* the first lunar landing mission.

Armstrong's companions on this historic flight were Lieutenant Colonel Michael Collins and Air Force Colonel Buzz Aldrin. Aldrin would be the lunar module pilot; Collins, the command module pilot.

On July 16, 1969, thousands of people jammed every available viewing space for miles around Kennedy Space Center. They were there to cheer on Armstrong, Aldrin, and

Neil Armstrong trains for his *Apollo 11* lunar landing mission at the Kennedy Space Center. His training pays off on July 20, 1969, when he becomes the first human being to set foot on the Moon.

Collins as they blasted off on the greatest trip in human history. They were not disappointed.

At precisely 9:32 A.M., the orange flame of ignition fired under *Apollo 11*'s mighty engines, followed by billowing clouds of smoke and steam. As the crowd screamed encouragement, the spacecraft began its slow, heart-pounding, ear-splitting climb toward the Moon, atop a thundering column of fire and smoke. When it disappeared from sight, people everywhere rushed to turn on their TV and radio sets, to continue following *Apollo*'s historic flight.

On July 19, the astronauts were in lunar orbit. On July 20, they were ready to descend to the Moon. Armstrong and Aldrin crawled into their lunar module, *Eagle,* and undocked from the command module, *Columbia.* As Collins continued to orbit in *Columbia,* the other two astronauts flew down toward the gray, desolate surface of the Moon.

Less than 200 feet above their target, the spacemen realized that the craft's automatic landing system was going to set them down in a crater littered with boulders. These rocks might tip the LM over, damage its landing gear, and leave them stranded on the Moon! With 114 seconds of fuel left for the landing phase of the journey, Armstrong made a bold decision. Instead of returning to *Columbia,* he took control of the LM and flew to a safer site.

At 4:16 P.M., 102 hours and 45 minutes after launch, he spoke to the world. His voice crackling as it traveled nearly a quarter of a million miles through space, he said, "Houston, Tranquility Base here. The *Eagle* has landed."

Armstrong was first out of the lunar module. As millions of people around the world watched and listened, his foot, encased in a heavy, size nine and a half boot, made the first footprint ever left in the powdery gray dust of the Moon.

Soon Aldrin joined him. Gaining confidence with every step, the two jumped and loped across the barren landscape for two hours and fourteen minutes. They performed experiments, collected Moon rocks, and planted an American flag as a reminder of their visit. They also received the longest long-distance telephone call in history: President Nixon called from the White House. Then it was time to go home. They reentered *Eagle* and returned to *Columbia.*

Splashdown came on July 24. *Columbia*'s jubilant crew was picked up by the aircraft carrier USS *Hornet.* Once aboard, the astronauts were hustled into an isolation trailer. Scientists feared they might be contaminated with Moon germs! During the eighteen-day isolation period, doctors discovered the astronauts were perfectly healthy, and future moonwalkers were not quarantined.

Neil Armstrong returned to a hero's welcome after his historic moonflight but soon slipped out of public view. Always a private man, he left NASA in 1971 to take a job teaching engineering at the University of Cincinnati. He taught until 1980 and now works as a private businessman.

The Moon still bears his footprints. In the windless, weatherless moonscape, scientists believe, those prints can stay, unchanged, for a million years.

Just home from their successful Moon landing, the crew of *Apollo 11* (from left to right, Neil Armstrong, Michael Collins, and Buzz Aldrin) spend the next eighteen days in an isolation trailer to avoid contaminating the Earth with suspected Moon germs. During their confinement, they had many visitors, including President Richard M. Nixon.

The *Skylab* Astronauts

Astronaut Joseph Kerwin floats effortlessly inside the *Skylab* space station in 1973. Pictures like this showed people, for the first time, what life in weightlessness was like.

"*Skylab* was America's first space station," the counselor continues. "It paved the way for the proposed future space station. The *Skylab* astronauts lived in it for long periods of time. And to the TV audiences who watched them, they looked as if they were having *fun!*"

Skylab 1 was a spin-off of the Apollo project. Launched, unmanned, on May 14, 1973, the orbiting house-sized space laboratory became the home for three separate crews whose mission was to find out whether human beings could adapt to long-term life and work in space. The astronauts rocketed up to *Skylab* in a leftover Apollo spacecraft, docked with it, and entered the space station through a connecting air lock. When their work was finished, they undocked and returned to Earth.

While in *Skylab,* the astronauts rode an exercise bike daily to keep fit. They floated around the orbital workshop in cleated shoes that locked into the metal grid of the floor; performed experiments; "cooked" meals in specially designed heating trays; and slept in closet-sized bedrooms, zipped into sleeping bags that attached to the walls.

The last crew left *Skylab* in February 1974. Gradually, the orbit of the abandoned station deteriorated, and on July 11, 1979, it plummeted back toward Earth. Most of it burned up in the heat of reentry, while the rest fell harmlessly into the Indian Ocean and over the sparsely populated Australian outback.

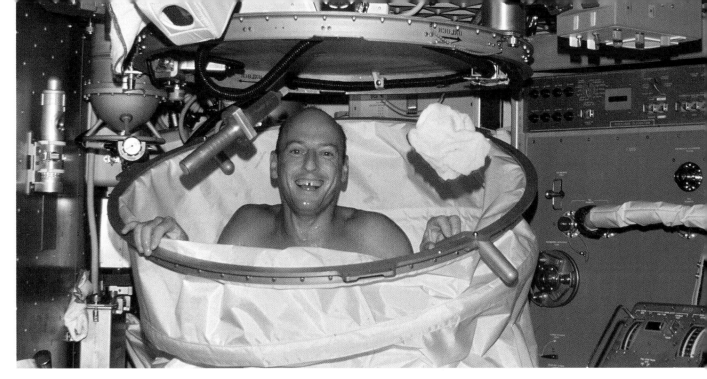

Skylab's commander, Charles Conrad, Jr., smiles after a hot shower in the crew's quarters.

Charles "Pete" Conrad, Jr.

"*Skylab* was in trouble when its first commander, Captain Pete Conrad, and his crew flew up to it," says Allyson. "The space station's protective shield had torn loose after lift-off. One solar panel was ripped off. The other was jammed."

Conrad's job was to rescue the project. The veteran of three spaceflights, and the third human to step on the Moon, during the *Apollo 12* flight of 1969, he now faced his biggest challenge. The loss of the heat shield exposed *Skylab* to the searing rays of the Sun. The loss of the power-generating solar panels meant that *Skylab* was operating on half the power it needed.

After docking with the space station, Conrad and his crewmates, Paul Weitz and Dr. Joseph Kerwin, deployed an emergency sunshade over *Skylab,* bringing its inside temperature down from 165° F to a balmy 80° F. Later, Conrad went outside to help unjam the damaged solar panel. This restored enough power to the space laboratory for the astronauts to settle down and lead a "normal" life in space.

Twenty-eight days and fifty minutes later, the three astronauts returned to Earth. Although they had all lost weight and were weakened and light-headed, they were undaunted. Emerging from the Apollo capsule on June 22, 1973, Conrad declared, "Everybody here is in super shape." And within two days, they felt normal again.

NASA was happy. If that was the worst that life in space could do, America would return. One day, a *permanent* space station would be built.

Pete Conrad retired from NASA in December 1973, after eleven years as an astronaut. A businessman now, he has received many awards, including the Congressional Space Medal of Honor.

The *Apollo-Soyuz* Astronauts

"The last Apollo mission was *Apollo-Soyuz,*" Allyson informs the Space Campers. "For the first time, the United States and the USSR worked together."

The *Apollo-Soyuz*'s mission was to develop and test a universal space docking system for the joint spaceflights of the future. When space travel becomes more common, a universal docking system would allow one nation's spacecraft to dock with another's, or any spaceship to berth at an international space station.

This cooperative space venture wasn't easy. America and the USSR still distrusted each other. In addition, there were differences to be resolved in space hardware, tracking systems, and techniques. And the language barrier only made it worse.

Each nation designed its own part of the linking device, but the central docking mechanism was created by both. For three years, battles between the two superpowers were fought and resolved. Finally, on July 15, 1975, the beginning of a new era of cooperation between former enemies was marked by a "handshake in space."

Astronaut Donald Slayton (right) and cosmonaut Valery Kubasov (left) practice in the docking module trainer at Houston's Johnson Space Center for the first joint Soviet-American mission.

Donald K. "Deke" Slayton

"Six of the Mercury Seven astronauts flew missions in the one-man spacecraft; Deke Slayton didn't," says Allyson.

Scheduled to be the second American to orbit the Earth, Slayton was grounded just two months before his expected launch because of a heart problem. The astronaut remained on Earth for the next thirteen years.

Despite the fact that his dream seemed more remote than the Moon, Slayton remained in the space program. He never became bitter or gave up. As head of the Astronaut Office in Houston, and later as director of flight crew operations, he became one of the most respected people at NASA. Perhaps his rugged childhood on a farm in Sparta, Wisconsin, during the 1920s toughened him for the long battle to fly into space.

In 1970, Slayton's heart unexpectedly returned to normal. Two years later, he was reassigned to active astronaut duty. His chances of getting an assignment were still slim, however. All the crews for the remaining lunar flights and *Skylab* missions had been picked. Only one Apollo mission remained: *Apollo-Soyuz.* Slayton wasn't going to miss *that* trip! Even before the United States and the Soviet Union signed their agreement, he began to study Russian.

On July 15, 1975, *Soyuz* took off from the USSR, piloted by cosmonauts Alexei Leonov and Valery Kubasov. Seven and a half hours later, *Apollo* blasted off from Kennedy Space Center. Among its three-man crew was fifty-one-year-old Slayton—the oldest American of that period ever to launch into space for the first time. Commander Thomas P. Stafford and Vance D. Brand completed NASA's team.

Two days after blast-off, *Apollo*'s crew sighted *Soyuz.* They inched toward the Soviet spacecraft, and with a gentle bump, the spaceships merged and locked together. Opening the door of the Russian capsule, Stafford cried out, "Tovarich!" (Friend!) "Very, very happy to see you!" Leonov replied.

For the next two days, the two crews performed a number of experiments together. When they were finished, they separated, linked again in a last test of the docking mechanism, then parted for good. *Soyuz* returned to the USSR; *Apollo* orbited for three more days before splashdown in the Pacific on July 24.

It was Apollo's, and Slayton's, last flight. The Apollo spacecraft was retired, but Slayton continued. He returned to NASA, where he became vitally involved in the early Space Shuttle testing programs. He retired from NASA in 1982 and went into private business. He died in 1993 at the age of sixty-nine.

During a lifetime of service to his country, Deke Slayton watched the astronaut corps grow from an elite band of seven military test pilots to a corps of almost two hundred men and women of different backgrounds and races. His single spaceflight set a standard for international cooperation that is bearing fruit today.

The First Space Shuttle Astronauts

"The Space Shuttle started a new era in space exploration," says Allyson. "It was a different time for astronauts, too. The group of thirty-five people NASA chose in 1978 included six women, three African-American men, and one Japanese-American man. Many of them were scientists and engineers instead of pilots. In the shirtsleeve environment of the Shuttle, they worked side by side, as equals."

The Shuttle was designed to be a "space bus" to carry people and materials back and forth between Earth and the permanent space station the United States plans to build with Canada, Europe, Japan, and Russia. The space station hasn't been built yet. But the Shuttle is hard at work.

The world's first reusable spacecraft launches like a rocket, orbits the Earth like a spaceship, and coasts home without engine power to sustain it, like a glider plane or bird. Both the orbiter, or space plane, and the solid-rocket boosters that help launch it into space are used over and over again. Only the external fuel tank is not recycled.

Since the Shuttle has no space station to go to yet, it has become an orbiting space laboratory, housing a crew of up to seven people. It also carries large payloads, or cargoes, of

Allyson shows the Apple team a model of the Space Shuttle located at the U.S. Space and Rocket Center in Huntsville, Alabama.

The crew of the *Challenger* mission of June 1983 show the jelly beans they discovered among their food supplies. The label on the bag Sally Ride is holding reads *Compliments of the White House*. (Jelly beans were President Ronald Reagan's favorite food.) From left to right, crew members are Sally K. Ride, Robert L. Crippen, Frederick H. Hauck, Norman E. Thagard, and John M. Fabian.

scientific experiments and satellites into space for countries, companies, and universities that pay to have their experiments performed and satellites launched.

Mission specialists are a new kind of astronaut. Full-time NASA astronauts, they know almost everything about the Shuttle's operation and spend time in flight training. They also perform most of the experiments, as well as deploy satellites into space and service and repair them.

Nonastronaut scientists, with little astronaut training, also go into space. Called payload specialists, they work for the countries, universities, or corporations whose scientific experiments they perform during a mission.

With a spacecraft largely controlled by sophisticated computers, only the commander and pilot *must* be able to fly the Shuttle. Anyone who is fit and healthy, is able to work well on a team, and has scientific or engineering skills that NASA needs may apply to be a mission specialist.

To command the first flight of *Columbia,* however, NASA turned to a seasoned veteran. With two Gemini and two Apollo spaceflights to his credit, Captain John W. Young was the most experienced astronaut in the world.

John W. Young

"Over 600,000 people came to Kennedy Space Center on April 12, 1981, to see John Young launch," says Allyson. "Nobody had ever seen anything like *Columbia* before."

The first commander of the Space Shuttle and the veteran of six spaceflights, John W. Young is said to be the world's most experienced astronaut.

The assembled three-part spaceship stood fourteen stories tall and weighed over 2,000 tons. The winged orbiter, clinging to the back of its external fuel tank (ET), and flanked by its two solid-rocket boosters (SRBs), gleamed with 32,000 ceramic heat tiles glued onto its aluminum skin. The tiles would shield the astronauts from the heat of reentry.

The mood was electric. Never before had American astronauts launched in a spacecraft that hadn't been tested first by an unmanned launch. How safe was *Columbia*? The astronauts' goals were simple: a safe flight and return to Earth.

Exactly twenty years after Yuri Gagarin's pioneering space journey, Young and his rookie pilot, Captain Robert L. Crippen, blasted off in a thunder of flame and smoke. Within six seconds, they cleared the launch tower. Two minutes later, the SRBs, their fuel spent, burst free from the ET. They parachuted into the Atlantic, where tugboats retrieved them and towed them back to land, to be refitted for flight.

A few minutes before orbit, the ET, its fuel exhausted, separated from the orbiter and fell toward the Indian Ocean, burning up as it reentered Earth's atmosphere. Then Young fired the two orbital maneuvering system (OMS) engines and placed *Columbia* in orbit 172 miles above Earth.

Making thirty-six Earth orbits over the next fifty-four and a half hours, the astronauts tested the spacecraft's systems. *Columbia* performed beautifully. Only one thing was wrong: A few heat tiles had fallen off, probably during launch. Would their loss hurt *Columbia* and her astronauts? Though NASA and people all over the world were frightened, the spacemen remained calm.

When it was time to come home, Young fired the OMS engines again to take the spacecraft out of orbit. He knew he would have only *one* chance to land the orbiter safely, at Edwards Air Force Base, in California's Mojave Desert.

John Young (left) and Robert Crippen (right) train for their upcoming mission aboard the world's first Space Shuttle, *Columbia*, in a mock-up of the real Shuttle's flight deck at Johnson Space Center. Young would be the commander of the untried spacecraft, and Crippen the pilot.

Columbia plummeted toward Earth, its black-tiled belly glowing bright orange as surface temperatures rose to 2,700° F. As the air grew denser, the spaceship became a glider plane. Young took over *Columbia*'s controls as the small attitude control engines shut down and the wing elevons, or flaps, and tail rudder began to work. Skillfully, he maneuvered the space plane through a series of S turns to slow its descent.

The Shuttle landed, rear wheels first. Hitting the dry lake bed of the desert at 215 miles an hour, it glided to a stop. *Columbia* was the first spacecraft to return to a runway landing.

Mission Control was ecstatic at the success of the spaceflight, despite the lost heat tiles. Young praised the brilliant performance of *Columbia* and its designers and builders, then went back to work.

Born in San Francisco, California, on September 24, 1930, John Young earned an aeronautical engineering degree from the Georgia Institute of Technology in 1952. He joined the navy and became a navy test pilot. Married to the former Susy Feldman, he and his wife have two children.

Chosen to be an astronaut in 1962, Young is the first person to fly in space six times and is one of six men who drove the Lunar Rover on the Moon. He now works at the Johnson Space Center, helping to keep the Space Shuttle running safely. He also advises on engineering and safety matters for the new Shuttle and the future space station.

Still an active astronaut at sixty-four, Young is eligible to command future Shuttle astronaut crews.

Sally Kristen Ride

"Sally Ride never wanted fame," Allyson continues. "But before she even left the Earth, she became the most famous American astronaut since Neil Armstrong. The U.S.'s first female astronaut, she opened NASA's doors to all the women who followed her."

"I did not come to NASA to make history," Ride once told a *Newsweek* reporter. "It's important to me that people don't think I was picked for the flight because I am a woman and it's time for NASA to send one." Nobody who knew her thought that.

By the time Sally Ride launched on June 18, 1983, the USSR had already sent two Soviet women into space: Valentina Tereshkova on June 16, 1963, and Svetlana Savitskaya on August 19, 1982. Tereshkova was a former textile mill worker who later graduated from the Zhukovskiy Air Force Engineering Academy and became an Honorary Colonel Engineer of the Soviet Air Force. Her single three-day flight, completed aboard *Vostok 6* with fellow cosmonaut Valery Bykov, gave her the honor of being the only woman in space for nineteen years. This record held until the flight of Svetlana Savitskaya, a test pilot and flight engineer, who flew aboard *Soyuz T-7* and became the first woman ever to make a spacewalk. A woman, however, had never flown in an American spacecraft. It really was time for NASA to follow suit.

Of the exceptional group of women chosen as mission specialists in 1978, Sally Ride was a standout. Born on May 26, 1951, in Los Angeles, California, she was one of two daughters of a political-science professor, Dr. Dale B. Ride, and his wife, Joyce. A talented athlete, Ride became a nationally ranked junior tennis player in her teens, and she could have turned professional. Instead, inspired by her high school physiology teacher, she chose a career in science.

She graduated from Stanford University in 1978, with degrees in both English and physics. Later, she earned a master's degree and a doctorate in physics.

Her academic background was perfect for the space program. So was her timing. She began job hunting in 1977, the year that NASA announced it was accepting applications for the first time since 1969, and that women would be considered. Until then, Ride said, "It hadn't occurred to me that it was even an option." She applied along with 1,000 other women and over 7,000 men. Nine months later, she began training as a mission specialist. Six years later, she rocketed into space aboard *Challenger.*

Ride's main job as flight engineer on her first mission was to help crewmate John M. Fabian operate the Shuttle's fifty-foot-long remote manipulator system (RMS). Developed in Canada, this robotic arm lies cradled within the left side of the payload bay until the orbiter is in space. Then the bay is opened, and the arm is deployed to help launch or retrieve satellites. Ride spent two years practicing with it.

Her years of work paid off. She used the arm deftly to help deploy and retrieve a German scientific package five times. (Work like this is important if astronauts are to help build a space station in the future.) She also helped place two commercial communica-

Which way is up? Astronaut Sally Ride eats a meal during her first space mission, in 1983. With her food tray Velcroed to her right leg, she seems glued to *Challenger*'s ceiling. Below her feet is the galley, where food is prepared.

tions satellites in orbit and performed experiments.

Ride's mission lasted six and a half days and was a triumph. Women everywhere were proud of her achievement. Gloria Steinem, a leader of the women's movement, said, "It's an important first because . . . millions and millions of little girls are going to sit in front of the television set and know they can become astronauts after this."

NASA flight director John Cox said, "She showed that she's just as capable as any of the men."

Sally Ride herself said simply, "I'm sure that it's the most fun I'll ever have in my life."

She flew in space once more, on STS 41-G, an eight-day mission aboard *Challenger*. Launched on October 5, 1984, it included the second American woman to fly into space, Dr. Kathryn D. Sullivan.

Ride was assigned as mission specialist for a third flight but stopped training in 1986, after the *Challenger* disaster killed seven of her fellow astronauts. She served as a member of the Presidential Commission exploring why the accident happened. When the investigation was over, she became special assistant to the administrator for long-range and strategic planning at NASA headquarters.

In 1987, Dr. Ride resigned from NASA and returned to Stanford University as a physicist. At present, she works as director of the California Space Institute at the University of California, San Diego.

Although she is no longer active in NASA's space program, the world won't forget her. When it came to being an astronaut, Ride's only question was, "Can I do the job?"

She could, and she did.

Guion S. Bluford, Jr.

"Just two months after Sally Ride's flight, there was another major breakthrough in the space program. Colonel Guion S. Bluford launched into space—the first African-American to do so. Colonel Bluford was a happy man. His childhood dreams were coming true."

Born November 22, 1942, in Philadelphia, Pennsylvania, Guy was the oldest of the three sons of Guion, Sr., and Lolita Bluford. Both parents had master's degrees and expected their children to go to college. Anything, they believed, was possible. They are Guy's heroes.

Guion S. Bluford was the first African-American in space. He blasted off aboard *Challenger* on August 30, 1983.

Like Neil Armstrong and John Glenn, Guy loved airplanes. He built model planes and as a paper boy tried different ways of folding and throwing the newspapers he delivered to see which way they flew the best. Gradually, it became clear to him. He didn't want to *fly* planes, he wanted to build them. He wanted to be an aerospace engineer!

His school guidance counselors at Overbrook High School thought he wasn't smart enough to do that. He excelled in math and science but was weak in reading. "Go to a technical school," they advised him, "and learn a trade instead."

Fortunately, the future astronaut ignored their advice. He enrolled at Pennsylvania State University and earned a degree in aerospace engineering. He married Linda Tull, and they had two sons. After graduating, he joined the air force. By 1967, he was flying combat missions over North Vietnam. A highly decorated fighter pilot, he logged over 5,200 hours of jet flying time before returning to the United States to become a pilot instructor and an assistant flight commander.

He earned a master's degree and a doctorate in aerospace engineering from the Air Force Institute of Technology and a master's in business administration from the University of Houston. To crown his achievements, he was one of 35 people NASA chose from a pool of nearly 9,000 applicants to join the eighth group of astronauts. For a boy who was told he wasn't college material, he had come a long way!

Though he strongly supports the aspirations of all African-American people and appreciates his importance to them, Bluford didn't join NASA simply to become a role model for others. He became an astronaut to achieve his dream of combining aerospace engineering with flying.

Bluford's first launch, on August 30, 1983, received worldwide attention. Although his parents were no longer living, his performance during the five-day mission justified their faith in him. During the flight, Mission Specialist Bluford helped deploy INSAT-1B, the $45 million Indian satellite that continues to provide communications and weather information to the subcontinent. He also did experiments with important medicines that may best be manufactured in space.

Other missions followed. A veteran of four spaceflights who logged over 688 hours in space, Bluford retired from NASA in 1993 to become a successful engineer and business executive. He knows that, like many astronauts, he has become a role model—not just for African-Americans, but for all young people with aspirations. "They can do whatever they want," he believes. "There aren't any barriers to hold them back. . . . If you really want to do something and are willing to put in the hard work it takes, then someday—bingo—you've done it!"

Guy Bluford works out in space on a stationary bicycle. A pressure cuff on his left arm monitors his heart rate as he exercises.

Sharon Christa Corrigan McAuliffe

"The world called her Christa," says Allyson, "even after she became the biggest space celebrity since Sally Ride. People loved her. She was everyone's dream of what a teacher should be."

Christa McAuliffe was the first of Edward and Grace Corrigan's five children. She was fearless. At three, she headed off downtown on her tricycle one Sunday morning, while her parents and dog, Teddy, were resting. The frantic Corrigans found her later, pedaling down the center of a busy street, with cars streaming past her in both directions.

Despite her adventurous spirit, Christa was a responsible, loving young woman. After graduating from Marian High School and Framingham State College, where she earned a bachelor's degree in history, she married her high school sweetheart, Steven James McAuliffe. She went to work as an American history teacher and had two children: Scott and Caroline. In 1978, she earned her master's degree in education. From then until 1985, she taught high school English and American history in Concord, New Hampshire.

While she was attending an annual meeting for social studies teachers in 1984, she saw a display of application packets from NASA, explaining the new Teacher-in-Space project. All teachers, provided they were American citizens with at least five years of successful classroom experience, were invited to apply for the job! The teachers didn't have to be superhuman, like the Mercury Seven. They didn't need advanced science or engineering degrees, like those of Guion Bluford and Sally Ride. And though each teacher had to come up with a mission project that he or she would carry out in space and broadcast to Earth over satellite TV, it didn't have to be high-tech.

The Teacher-in-Space project sounded great to the adventurous thirty-six-year-old mother of two. And Christa's simple project—writing a diary of her space experiences— plus her fresh, lively personality, seemed great to NASA. The space agency picked her from a group of 11,500 eager applicants.

Christa sailed through her six months of NASA training, buoyed by her self-confidence and the support of her family. Launch day finally arrived on January 28, 1986. Lift-off of STS 51-L had been delayed six times because of bad weather and technical malfunctions. On January 28, though, a team of inspectors examined the Shuttle one last time. Despite a record 25° F cold front, which had caused icicles to form on the launch tower, it was decided that everything was fine.

As Christa and her six crewmates—Francis R. Scobee, Michael J. Smith, Ellison S. Onizuka, Judith A. Resnik, Ronald E. McNair, and Greg Jarvis—waited to go, people all over the world tuned in. Children in classrooms throughout America assembled in front of TV sets to watch a teacher fly into space.

The SRBs fired, and the Shuttle *Challenger* rose on a thick cloud of billowing smoke in the frozen air. Seventy-three seconds into flight, the Shuttle disintegrated. All astronauts, including Christa, were killed.

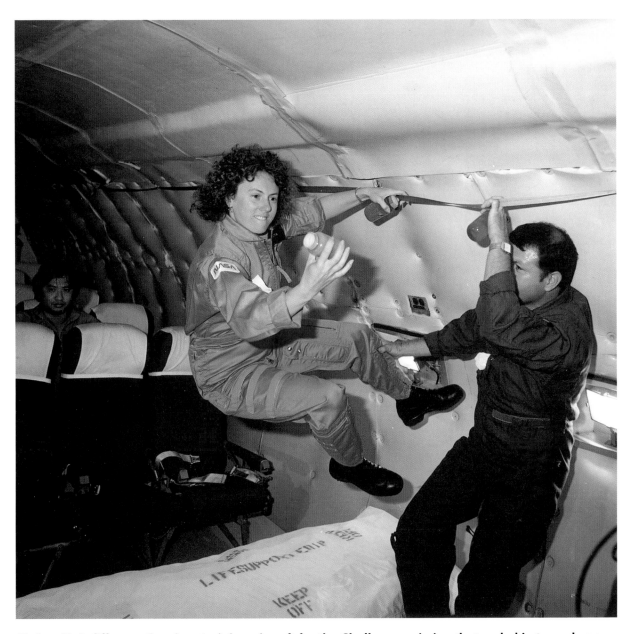

Christa McAuliffe practices in a training aircraft for the _Challenger_ mission that ended in tragedy on January 28, 1986. The two jars she holds contain a mixture of oil and water. In the few moments of weightlessness she experiences when the aircraft dives, she sees that the liquids separate differently in zero gravity from the way they do on Earth.

An intense investigation followed. No more Shuttles launched for almost two and a half years, until NASA was satisfied that the spacecraft and launch procedures were as safe as possible.

Christa McAuliffe continues to touch people's lives. Scholarships and memorials have been established in her name, and the Christa McAuliffe Planetarium opened in Concord in 1990. Her mother, Grace Corrigan, expressed Christa's legacy to children everywhere: "[She] is a real hero because she actually did with her life what each of us is capable of doing with our own. . . . Christa _lived._ She never just sat back and existed."

International and Current Shuttle Astronauts

"Astronauts have changed since 1959," Allyson states. "During the Mercury, Gemini, and Apollo periods, they were all white male test pilots. With the Space Shuttle came men and women of different backgrounds, with scientific, medical, and engineering skills. International astronauts are the latest development. They are working with American astronauts on the projects of the future: a space station, a lunar base, and missions to distant planets, such as Mars."

The crew of the first joint Russian-American Spacehab mission, of February 3, 1994, pose for a picture. N. Jan Davis is in the center. Circling her from left to right are Franklin Chang-Diaz; Sergei Krikalev; Kenneth S. Reightler, Jr.; Charles F. Bolden, Jr.; and Ronald M. Sega.

Mamoru Mohri

"Mamoru Mohri was the eighth child of a veterinarian and his wife who lived in Yoichi, Hokkaido—the northernmost island of Japan. He was born after World War II, on January 29, 1949. Because his father was an animal doctor, the family had many pets: dogs, cats, rabbits, chickens, goats, and fish."

When Mamoru was twelve years old, Yuri Gagarin made his historic flight. Watching the Russian cosmonaut on TV, the boy formed a secret ambition. Until that moment, he had always wanted to be a scientist. Now he also dreamed of being an astronaut.

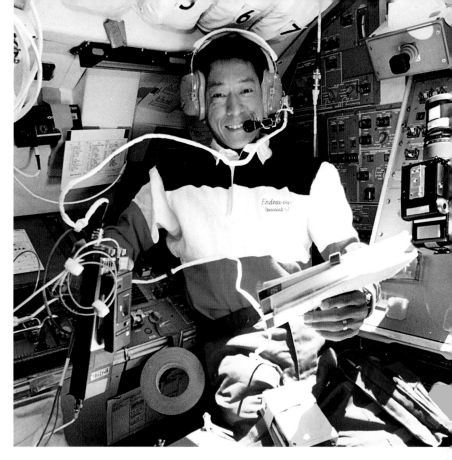

Japanese astronaut Mamoru Mohri talks from space with students in Japan during the first joint Japanese-American Spacelab-J mission, September 12, 1992.

He continued to follow a path in science, however. Encouraged by his high school chemistry teacher, he went to Hokkaido University, where he earned a bachelor's and a master's degree in chemistry. After completing a doctorate in chemistry, he joined the faculty of Hokkaido University, where he taught nuclear engineering. He is married to the former Akiko Naka and is the father of three children.

In 1985, NASDA, the National Space Development Agency of Japan, chose him as a payload specialist for the first joint Japanese-American space mission, launched on September 12, 1992. During the eight-day flight of *Endeavour,* Dr. Mohri performed forty-three experiments in material and life sciences with his NASA teammates. While in orbit, he also held a twenty-minute question-and-answer period about his life and work in space, beamed from the Shuttle to a group of elementary and high school students in Japan. The interview was a nationwide event in his country, and Mohri, like so many astronauts before him, found that he had become a national celebrity.

Currently working as general manager of the recently founded NASDA Astronaut Office in Tsukuba Science City, Japan, Dr. Mohri has been assigned to develop Japan's astronaut program for the proposed Japanese-American-European-Russian space station.

Does he suggest the life of an astronaut to today's young people? Absolutely. "I highly recommend that those who dream of a career in space *live* their dream. The job of astronaut is a very rewarding one."

N. Jan Davis

"'If you aim high, you'll never hit low!' Jan Davis's mother used to say," says Allyson.

"Jan took those words to heart. When she grew up, she aimed for a career that would take her higher and farther than most people will ever go. And she worked hard to get there. On September 12, 1992, her work paid off. Dr. N. Jan Davis blasted into space aboard STS-47, NASA's fiftieth Space Shuttle mission. How's that for aiming high?"

Born on November 1, 1953, in Cocoa Beach, Florida, Jan moved to Huntsville, Alabama—the home of the U.S. Space and Rocket Center—when she was in the fifth grade. She had a happy, active childhood, complete with braces on her teeth, a younger

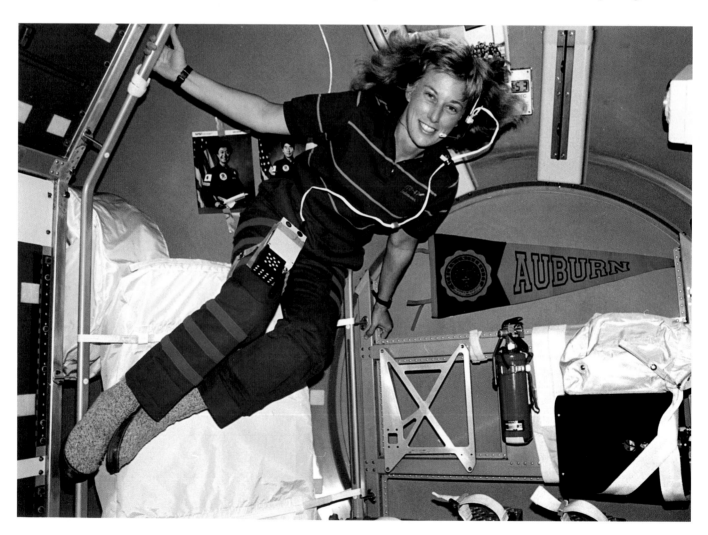

Jan Davis floats in front of a pennant honoring her alma mater, Auburn University, during the flight of STS-47, *Endeavour,* in 1992. The photographs behind her are of the two backup payload specialists for Spacelab-J, Drs. Chiaki Mukai and Takao Doi, who trained for but did not actually fly on the mission, since Mamoru Mohri went up instead.

brother named Ron, and a pair of family dogs called Flopsy and Susu. Her hobbies included sewing, crafts, piano, dancing, softball, and cheerleading. Encouraged by her parents and teachers, she loved school—especially math and science. "I was always excited in August when school supplies came out in the stores," the astronaut recalls. "I enjoyed learning."

There was never any question that she would go on to college. After graduating from Huntsville High School in 1971, she earned a degree in applied biology from the Georgia Institute of Technology in 1975 and another in mechanical engineering from Auburn University in 1977. Continuing on, she acquired a master of science degree in 1983, then a doctorate in mechanical engineering two years later, from the University of Alabama.

In 1978, after NASA selected its first group of women mission specialists, Davis began thinking of a career in space herself. She started by working as an aerospace engineer for NASA's Marshall Space Flight Center in 1979. Among her many assignments there was being the leader of a team working on the Hubble Space Telescope.

Beginning in 1984, she applied three times to become an astronaut. Twice, she didn't make it. But her persistence, educational background, and reputation as a hardworking, well-rounded team player impressed NASA. In 1987 she was chosen!

Over the five years that passed between being picked as a mission specialist and her first launch, Dr. Davis had many important jobs, including working with Shuttle crews as a spacecraft communicator (CAPCOM) in Houston's Mission Control.

On September 12, 1992, she launched into space herself aboard the Shuttle *Endeavour*, on STS-47, Spacelab-J, the first joint Japanese-American space mission. During this eight-day flight, she was responsible for operating Spacelab and for performing a number of the mission's forty-three experiments.

She was also a mission specialist on STS-60 (Spacehab), the first joint Russian-American venture, which launched aboard the Space Shuttle *Discovery* on February 3, 1994. Davis was responsible for maneuvering a new free-flying space platform called the Wake Shield Facility (WSF), using the Shuttle's robotic arm. She also performed experiments in the space habitation module.

So far, Davis has logged 289 hours in space. As an active astronaut, she will probably log many more. She likes being an astronaut because she loves flying and learning new things.

Like her mother before her, Jan Davis encourages young people to aim high and to do their very best to accomplish their goals. While a strong believer in education, the astronaut also wants children to have fun. "Do sports, hobbies, music. Don't just study all of the time!"

Franklin Chang-Diaz

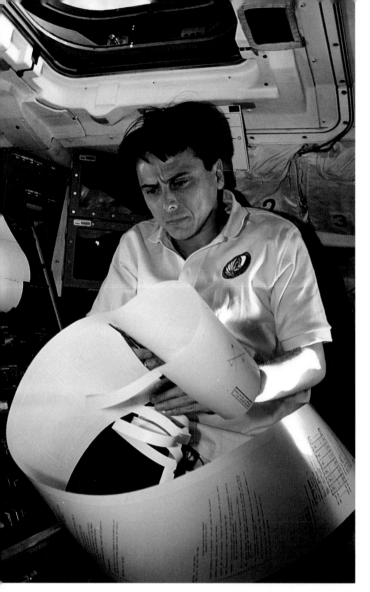

One of the longest mail messages in Space Shuttle history is studied by Franklin Chang-Diaz during an eight-day mission aboard *Discovery* in 1994. Four days of correspondence unfurl in the spacecraft.

"When the Soviet Union launched *Sputnik* into space in 1957, the news reached the remotest corners of the Earth," says Allyson.

On the edge of a rain forest in Venezuela, a seven-year-old Costa Rican boy named Franklin Chang-Diaz heard about it from his mother. "A new star made by people is circling the Earth," she said. Excited by this extraordinary event, Franklin scrambled into his tree house to watch the man-made star pass by. He stayed there for hours.

"I'm not sure I *really* saw it," says Dr. Chang-Diaz. "But that night, my dream was born. I thought I'd like to be a space explorer. Even though, at that time, there were no astronauts, I thought, Someday, there'll be some. I'd like to be one of them."

Once he graduated from high school in Costa Rica, he decided to go to school in the United States to become an American-trained scientist—as a first step on his path into space. In 1968, he left his country with fifty dollars in his wallet and a one-way plane ticket. Distant relatives in Hartford, Connecticut, let him live with them for a while.

After a year at Hartford High School, learning English, he won a scholarship to the University of Connecticut, where he earned a mechanical engineering degree. He won another scholarship to the Massachusetts Institute of Technology and graduated with a doctorate in applied plasma physics. That same year, 1977, he became a naturalized American citizen. He married Peggy Marguerite Doncaster, and they have three daughters.

Chang-Diaz was chosen as an astronaut candidate by NASA in May 1980 and became a full-fledged astronaut in August 1981. "When I called my father in San Jose to tell him the news, he cried," the astronaut remembers. "He always believed in me, but he wasn't sure I'd make it. I was the first Hispanic person chosen by NASA."

Chang-Diaz has flown four spaceflights now: the STS-61C mission of 1986, STS-34 in 1989, STS-46 in 1992, and the STS-60 mission of 1994. He has logged 656 hours in space and is still an active astronaut.

Mark C. Lee

"Can you imagine an astronaut who grew up on a mink ranch?" Allyson asks the team. "Well, Colonel Mark Lee did. He was born on August 14, 1952, in Viroqua, Wisconsin. His parents ran the ranch, but their six children, led by Mark, were expected to help take care of over 5,000 mink! He learned to work hard—and great things came from that."

While Mark was in third grade, Alan Shepard rocketed into space. After that, the boy from Wisconsin knew he wanted to be an astronaut when he grew up. But he was practical as well as hardworking. First, he would become a pilot and civil engineer. That way, he would have interesting work to do, even if his dream of space didn't work out.

School was quite easy for him. Like most future astronauts, Mark excelled at math and science. He also loved sports. Graduating from Viroqua High School in 1970, he earned a degree in civil engineering from the U.S. Air Force Academy in 1974 and a master's degree in mechanical engineering from MIT in 1980. He became an air force lieutenant colonel, logging 3,500 hours of flying time in some of the fastest aircraft in the world.

Chosen as an astronaut candidate in May 1984, Lee first launched on May 4, 1989, as a mission specialist on STS-30. He also flew as payload commander on STS-47, Spacelab-J, the first joint Japanese-American mission, launched September 12, 1992.

On September 9, 1994, Lee flew into space a third time, on STS-64. This time, he performed his first spacewalk, testing a new jet pack developed by NASA. Called SAFER, for Simplified Aid for Extravehicular Activity Rescue, it is not nearly as thick or clumsy as the massive MMU (Manned Maneuvering Unit) used by the six previous astronauts who walked in space without being tethered to the spacecraft. The astronaut straps on SAFER like a backpack and guides it by using a joystick.

Lee's spacewalk helped to prove that the compact jet pack can do what it was designed to do: help rescue space station crews of the future, if they become separated from the station.

Colonel Lee has spent almost 551 hours in space. An active astronaut, he is likely to add to that score as he continues in what he calls "the greatest job in the universe!"

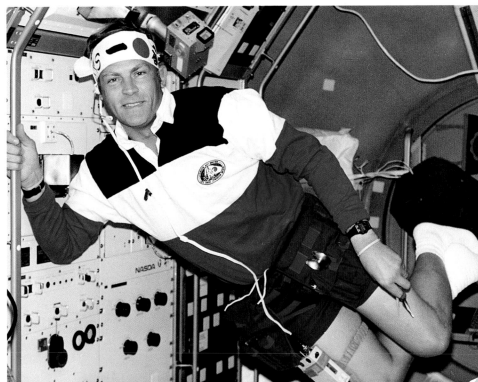

The headband worn by Mark Lee has Japanese characters on it that spell *ichiban,* meaning "number one." Since Lee was mission specialist 1 on the Japanese-American Spacelab-J mission of 1992, he added *M.S.* to the band.

Young Astronauts Look to the Future

Apple team and Allyson are waiting to meet Colonel R. Mike Mullane, a veteran of three spaceflights and this summer's astronaut-in-residence at Space Camp. Colonel Mullane has retired from NASA and the air force to become a writer. The children are eager to hear him.

Former astronaut Mike Mullane, now a speaker and published author, talks to Space Campers about the future of space exploration.

While they wait, Allyson tries to answer a camper's question: "How can I become an astronaut?"

"It's hard," she says. "Only one in thousands of applicants makes it. Still, I may apply myself in a few years. NASA needs pilot astronauts and mission specialists for its Shuttle program. It takes applications all the time and chooses new candidates every two years, as spaces open."

"Can anyone apply?"

"Both civilians and people in the military services can apply. But you have to be a United States citizen to be an American astronaut."

"Do you have to be really strong?"

"No, but you should be in top physical condition, with a great education. Mission specialists and pilot astronauts need at least a bachelor's degree in engineering, biological science, physical science, or mathematics from an accredited college or university. And you have to have worked for at least three years in your special field after graduating. Advanced degrees are helpful, and good grades are important!"

"What about pilots?" asks a girl who would like to fly a Shuttle.

"Pilot astronauts need at least 1,000 hours of flying experience in jet aircraft. And they should have excellent eyesight."

"How soon does NASA tell you whether you made it as an astronaut?" calls out a boy.

"NASA chooses astronauts after they successfully complete a one-year training and evaluation period."

The team has more questions, but Allyson gives the children a suggestion instead. "For information, you can do what I did. Write to the Astronaut Selection Office, NASA Johnson Space Center, Houston, Texas 77058. Check it out yourself!"

As the campers write this down in their logbooks, Colonel Mullane arrives. A slender, friendly man, he has lived a life of risk and adventure that few outside the astronaut corps can imagine. He tells the campers about himself.

"As a child," he begins, "I constantly looked to the sky. There was never any doubt about what I wanted to do with my life. I wanted to fly. Higher, faster than anyone else."

He tells the campers about his first flight—aboard *Discovery* on August 30, 1984—and the awesome moment of lift-off, when the Shuttle finally burst free of the pull of gravity. He tells of the fun he had, chasing a floating globule of liquid juice around the orbiter cabin and capturing it. He answers questions: "Were you ever afraid?"

"Of course. But I still wanted to do it more than anything else in the world."

The campers want to hear more about space. They know that humans have walked on the Moon and that unmanned spacecraft have visited all of the known nine planets in our solar system except Pluto. They know that the Earth is now orbited by communications and weather satellites, which relay voices, pictures, and information around the globe—almost instantaneously. Human beings, they know, have learned about how to live and work in space, and are still learning. They know there are plans to build a space station, to revisit the Moon and build a lunar base, and to travel to Mars. What they don't know is whether these projects will actually happen. Can *they* have careers in space, too?

The astronaut laughs. "The exploration of space has just begun!"

The Russian Space Agency has joined the United States, Japan, Europe, and Canada in the space station project. Having occupied space almost continually for the past twenty-three years, Russia brings special experience to the effort. Construction of the station is supposed to begin in the late 1990s. Already, American astronauts are training with Russian cosmonauts, preparing to dock NASA Shuttles with *MIR*, the world's only space station at present. Once it is built, the new station will replace the Space Shuttle as an orbiting space laboratory. Station astronauts will perform experiments, test new robot technology, and keep studying the effects of long-duration flight on human beings. Without such knowledge, it would be risky to venture much farther.

While the space station takes shape, teams of scientists and engineers will work on new, less costly ways to lift machinery and humans into orbit. One day, astronauts may ride into space aboard one of several new experimental transportation systems being developed, including America's National Aerospace Plane (NASP). The NASP will take off and land on a runway like a plane but will be able to fly into space like the Shuttle.

And in the twenty-first century, America and its partners hope to fly beyond Earth orbit again, first to the Moon, and then to Mars. When the first lunar base is built, it will be a remote outpost where astronauts, with the help of robotic workers, build life-support systems and conduct mining operations on the Moon. Eventually, we will continue on to Mars. Unmanned spacecraft and robots will explore the Martian surface first, before humans attempt to go there.

Future astronauts may travel around the Moon on a lunar utility vehicle (LUV) such as the one in this painting. A kind of space helicopter, the LUV will take off and land vertically, and skim above the rugged Moon terrain.

To reach distant planets faster, a new generation of rockets, using new energy sources, will need to be created. A trip to Mars would take a *year* using rockets like those of Saturn, which burned liquid oxygen and hydrogen to launch astronauts to the Moon! And for long space journeys, we may also need to create artificial gravity within the spacecraft, so that humans will remain healthy and strong enough to work when they reach their destination.

What does this mean to the young people of today? Colonel Mullane asks. Opportunity. "There could be a future for *you* in the space program. Not just as an astronaut, but as an engineer or scientist working on the frontier of human knowledge."

Before Mullane leaves, he tells the children a story about his grandmother, to illustrate how fast the field of space exploration has grown. "She was born in 1897 and traveled by covered wagon from Minnesota to Oklahoma when she was a baby. At the age of eighty-seven, she was standing on a beach in Florida near Kennedy Space Center—watching me blast into space. Who knows what your grandmothers and grandfathers may live to see? Within the next forty or fifty years, one of *you* may go to Mars. Or help create the technology to make such wonders possible. Think about it. The future is coming—and it belongs to you."

Bibliography

In addition to numerous NASA publications, such as *Former NASA Astronaut Biographies; Current NASA Astronaut Biographies; Current and Former Payload Specialists;* and *NASA Information Summaries: Astronaut Fact Book,* the following newspapers and magazines were particularly helpful: *The New York Times, Life, Time, Newsweek, U.S. News & World Report, Aviation Week, Air & Space, Final Frontier, Reader's Digest, Science Digest, Ms., Ebony, McCall's,* and *Macleans.*

The following books were also important:

Booth, Nicholas, and Brian Todd. *The Encyclopedia of Space.* New York: Mallard Press, 1989.

Contemporary Black Biography. Volume 1. 1991. Detroit: Gale Research.

Corrigan, Grace George. *A Journal for Christa.* Lincoln: University of Nebraska Press, 1993.

Crocker, Chris. *Great American Astronauts.* New York: Franklin Watts, 1988.

Current Biography. Volume 54, Number 7. July 1993. New York: H. W. Wilson.

De Ward, E. John, and Nancy De Ward. *History of NASA: America's Voyage to the Stars.* New York: Exeter Books, 1984.

Gurney, Gene. *Americans to the Moon.* New York: Random House, 1970.

Haskins, Jim, and Kathleen Benson. *Space Challenger: The Story of Guion Bluford.* Minneapolis: Carolrhoda Books, 1984.

Hohler, Robert T. *I Touch the Future: The Story of Christa McAuliffe.* New York: Random House, 1986.

Holden, William G., and William D. Siuru, Jr. *Skylab: Pioneer Space Station.* Chicago: Rand McNally, 1974.

Kerrod, Robin. *The Illustrated History of Man in Space.* New York: Mallard Press, 1989.

Life in Space. Alexandria, VA: Time-Life Books, 1983.

Ride, Sally, with Susan Okie. *To Space & Back.* New York: Lothrop, Lee & Shepard Books, 1986.

The Software Toolworks Illustrated Encyclopedia. Novato, CA: Grolier Electronic Publishing, 1990.

Von Riper, Frank. *Glenn: The Astronaut Who Would Be President.* New York: Empire Books, 1983.

Westman, Paul. *Neil Armstrong: Space Pioneer.* Minneapolis: Lerner Publications Company, 1980.

Wolfe, Tom. *The Right Stuff.* New York: Farrar, Straus, 1979.

From the NASA Film/Video Catalog at Johnson Space Center, these videos made the space adventure come alive:

Apollo 11: *For All Mankind.* 1975.

Astro Smiles. 1988.

Eagle *Has Landed: The Flight of* Apollo 11. 1969.

Four Rooms, Earth View. 1975.

Friendship 7: Flight of John Glenn. 1962.

Gemini VIII: *This Is Houston, Flight.* 1966.

GT-III: First Manned Gemini Mission. 1965.

Mission of Apollo-Soyuz. 1975.

Shuttle Life in the World of Weightlessness. 1987.

Skylab: *Space Station 1.* 1974.

Space Shuttle: A Remarkable Flying Machine. 1982.

Time of Apollo. 1975.

We Deliver. 1983.

World Was There. Rereleased 1975.

NASA-videotaped postmission press conferences were also valuable.

The IMAX space films *Destiny in Space,* 1994; *The Blue Planet,* 1990; *The Dream Is Alive,* 1985; and *Hail, Columbia,* May 1982, gave an astronaut's vision of what it is like now, and will be like in the future, to explore the worlds beyond our world.

Index